If I had a Monster

by David E. McAdams

Copyright 2025 David E. McAdams. All Rights Reserved.
No part of this work may be copied, stored or transmitted by any means without the express written consent of the copyright holder.

Other Books by David E. McAdams

Parrot Colors – A delightful introduction to colors featuring vibrant images of parrots. Perfect for ages 0-6.

Flower Colors – Explore the beauty of colors through captivating images of flowers. Ideal for ages 0-6.

Space Colors – Discover colors through stunning NASA space images. Suitable for ages 0-6.

People Colors – Introduces the concept of colors using diverse images of people from around the world. For ages 0-6.

If I Had a Monster – A charming story where monsters represent important people in a child's life. Fun for all ages.

Shapes – A playful introduction to geometric shapes, designed for children aged 3-6.

Numbers – A beginner-friendly book introducing the concept of numbers. Recommended for ages 5-7.

Red Neck Number Book – A humorous and engaging way to learn numbers in a unique style. Great for ages 2-6.

What is Bigger Than Anything? (Infinity) – A fascinating look at the concept of infinity for curious minds aged 6-8.

Swing Sets (Set Theory) – A comprehensive introduction to set theory, tailored for students aged 7-10.

One Penny, Two – Join Jerry on his journey to buy a sports car as his penny doubles each day. A captivating read for ages 8-12.

Learning With Play Money Activity Kit – A fun hands-on kit to teach counting and large numbers with over $2,000,000 in play money. Best for ages 8-12.

My Favorite Fractals (Volumes 1 & 2) – A visual treat of high-resolution fractal images, appealing to all ages.

Even Generals Take Out the Garbage – A heartwarming story that teaches children the importance of doing chores. Suitable for young readers.

All Math Words Dictionary – A comprehensive math dictionary covering key concepts in pre-algebra, algebra, geometry, and pre-calculus.

The First Million Digits of Pi – A book containing the first million digits of pi, fascinating for math enthusiasts of all ages.

The First Million Digits of e – A collection of the first million digits of Euler's number (e). Engaging for all ages.

The Square Root of 2 to One Million Digits – Explore the first million digits of the square root of 2. For curious minds of all ages.

The First Hundred Thousand Prime Numbers – A handy reference featuring the first hundred thousand prime numbers, suitable for all ages.

Geometric Nets Project Book – Contains 80 geometric nets to copy, cut out, and assemble into 3D polyhedra. Ideal for ages 9 and up.

Geometric Nets Mega Project Book – Features 253 geometric nets to copy, cut out, and construct into 3D polyhedra. Suitable for ages 9 and up.

For an up-to-date list of books, visit https://www.DEMcAdams.com.

Parents' Guide

In this book, monsters represent family members who do things with your child. You can help your child relate these monsters to people they know. Some questions might be:

- Who cuddles with you? How are they like the soft, cuddly monster who cuddles with you?
- Do you get sticky-faced when you eat ice cream? Who else gets sticky-faced when they eat ice cream?
- Do you have a sixteen year old monster to drive for you? What would it be like having a sixteen year old monster to drive for you?

If I had a monster, then it would be,
a soft fuzzy monster to cuddle with me.

If I had a monster, then it would be,
a fashion monster to play dress up with me.

If I had a monster, then it would be,
a cooking monster to make breakfast with me.

If I had a monster, then it would be,
a big silly monster to play games with me.

If I had a monster, then it would be,
a really smart monster to count raisins with me.

If I had a monster, then it would be,
a big eared monster to bang pots with me.

If I had a monster, then it would be,
a chef hatted monster to make cookies with me.

If I had a monster, then it would be,
a patient monster to do timeouts with me.

If I had a monster, then it would be,
a big mouthed monster to sing with me.

If I had a monster, then it would be,
a green faced to monster to color with me.

If I had a monster, then it would be,
a big ugly monster to scare brother and me.

If I had a monster, then it would be,
 a slippery monster to slide with me.

If I had a monster, then it would be,
a winged monster to fly with me.

If I had a monster, then it would be,
a bouncy monster to jump with me.

If I had a monster, then it would be,
a sixteen year old monster to drive for me.

If I had a monster, then it would be,
a tall tall monster to help me see.

If I had a monster, then it would be,
a monster truck monster to get dirty with me.

If I had a monster, then it would be,
a strong-strong monster to skip rocks with me.

If I had a monster, then it would be,
a mechanical monster to fix cars with me.

If I had a monster, then it would be,
a long armed monster to climb trees with me.

If I had a monster, then it would be,
an armored monster to play forts with me.

If I had a monster, then it would be,
a sticky faced monster to eat ice cream with me.

If I had a monster, then it would be,
a floaty monster to swim with me.

If I had a monster, then it would be,
a hungry monster to eat dinner with me

If I had a monster, then it would be,
a big toothed monster to brush teeth with me.

If I had a monster, then it would be,
a water monster to take baths with me.

If I had a monster, then it would be,
a no snoring monster to sleep with me.

www.ingramcontent.com/pod-product-compliance
Lightning Source LLC
LaVergne TN
LVHW072006060526
838200LV00010B/293